Reflections on Salvation

Reflections on Salvation

Kiriti Sengupta

TRANSCENDENT ZERO PRESS

Published in the United States of America in July, 2016 by Dustin Pickering and Zachary Weiss, at Transcendent Zero Press, 16429 EL Camino Real Apt. #7, Houston, Texas 77062-5786

Email: Editor@transcendentzeropress.org
Website: www.transcendentzeropress.org

Cover concept, illustration & design: Sourish Mitra

ISBN-13: 978-0-9962704-6-5

Library of Congress Control Number: 2016948357

Price: US Dollars 8.00
             INR 180/-

Dedicated to my beloved friend,
a brilliant story-writer, Bitan Chakraborty.

Foreword

Spirituality has always been a concept that has troubled me. As an atheist who views humans as but one part of a larger environment encompassing not just this world, but the universe beyond, who believes that nonviolence in action, speech and thought is a noble virtue and perhaps the only one that can save our world, I have been called "spiritual." I have rejected that term because I am a thoroughgoing materialist. I believe in matter and energy and that they are related. I believe that we understand them through science and that they are capable of being completely understood by humans (unless the relationship is so mathematically sophisticated that our brains can't comprehend it). I have no evidence, nor do I believe in conscious energy beyond that produced by animal brains (though I don't rule out plant consciousness as a possibility, but it would require an expansion of the concept of consciousness). My views on morality and ethics were shaped by my Christian upbringing, although, like Thomas Jefferson (my thoughts on a tiny and shabbier scale than his), I value the teachings of Christ but reject his status as a deity and I fully expect that I would find equally valuable moral lessons in the teachings of other religions, if I studied them.

So when the concept of spirituality is raised, I have to consider it seriously, but with great skepticism. Those who raise it do so sincerely and are neither to be mocked nor dismissed lightly. Their sincerity demands my respectful attention, though not my agreement.

Kiriti Sengupta has the some of the same problems I do with the concept of "salvation." His beautiful small book, Reflections on Salvation, wrestles with the conflict between the strict scriptural (i.e. *The Geeta*) interpretation of salvation and a more cosmopolitan, relativistic view of salvation that recognizes that it may represent different things for different people, including the massive number of people who seek or find salvation without having ever read *The Geeta*. He also reflects upon the concept of "renunciation" as part of the quest for salvation and whether it contains built-in hypocrisy and is perhaps inferior to attachment to the real world, to one's loved ones, and to the fruits of one's actions.

Sengupta faces these questions courageously, with poetic inspiration, and often with humor. As he hints in his introduction, he is also braving the criticism of religious scholars and the devout, who may view his reflections as heretical. Nevertheless, he forges ahead with a Cartesian-like zeal for doubting anything that is capable of being reduced only to authority and not to reason.

If monks distinguish themselves from the masses by wearing saffron robes, does this act of drawing attention to their uniqueness by their dress, constitute renunciation or attachment? In this and other passages, Sengupta reveals and criticizes hypocrisy. Even more so, he exposes the lack of connection between real-life issues that threaten our world, and the historical scriptural passages, unchanged to meet the crises of a world threatened by environmental issues, by malnutrition, etc. To be timeless, the words must be detached from worldliness, but does such detachment meet people's needs?

Mostly, the message of Sengupta's reflections is that belief in the value of the results of one's actions is both necessary and superior to withdrawal from such consequences into scripturally defined purity of spiritual consciousness. The person who kills creates real consequences—for others and for him or her self—regardless of whether or not he or she is "motivated by false ego." The one who plants fruit does so in order to eat them. He should aspire to eating them. *"Why won't I dream of eating mangoes if I plant or even intend to plant a mango tree?"* And what I found most refreshing, and even astounding, was his statement, *"Salvation is but enlightenment, achievable only by actions, and through your sensory gateways."* If you strive, but don't accomplish, can you claim to have achieved your outcome? If it were all in your mind, or in the following of scriptural prescriptions, perhaps you could, but, as Sengupta asks, *"did you deliver your best?"* Real salvation comes from real accomplishments, which come from real effort.

In the end, I find (and here I must guard against projection of my own values, so take my words with a grain of salt) that Sengupta's message is an expression of the spirituality of faith in the material world.

> *"We live as long as we breathe; and it is but the breathing which occurs on its own will. No gods, but the breath that builds a home for our life and death.*
> *They say, God dwells within; it is then the mortal exploration of the resort where salvation is largely seen."*

Casey Dorman
July 11, 2016
Editor, *Lost Coast Review*
California, United States of America

Have You Secured a Happy Afterlife?

The concluding chapter of *The Geeta* is titled "Moksha Yoga." *Moksha* is derived from the Sanskrit *Muc* that means *mukti* or salvation. Scriptures suggest that salvation is but coming out of the vicious circle of birth and death. What if someone does not believe in reincarnation at all?

Ask a writer, and they would probably say that it is their writing that allows them to taste liberation. Ask an actor, and they would possibly tell you that it is performance or acting that sets them free. You may ask an artist and you would understand that it is their creativity that makes them feel relieved. Who has seen a life beyond death? I am asking you, for I have not witnessed one myself.

Kaushik Acharya, a friend, who teaches Sanskrit in a government-aided school and doing doctoral research in Sanskrit literature in Jadavpur University (Calcutta), was sitting beside me as I intended to write an introduction to my poetic prose pieces. He said, "If you don't believe in re-birth at all, don't you dare to think or use "salvation."" I questioned his intention and said, "Why? Is "salvation" a word meant only for the followers of the scriptures? *Mukti* or "salvation" might carry various meanings to varied people." Kaushik argued, "If you think so, you have not understood the meaning of *moksha* in the first place." He was perhaps focused on the literal meaning of *moksha*, but *I'm no linguist/ I know air and age/ are linked/ since eternity./ And the wounds surface again/ in all directions.../ sporting the guise of youth.* [Ref: *Healing Waters Floating Lamps*]

Kaushik read a few pieces from the collection and remarked on them, "We call it misinterpretation of scripture! You must be strong enough to take the flak if your work is reviewed by a scholar." "But then, mine is not a scholastic work by any means," I made my point clear to my friend.

The Geeta has been interpreted by many scholars, saints and monks down the ages. One considers another wrong or bad. One interpretation invites another, and it has been observed that what once had been referred to as a right interpretation, has later been criticized as a misinterpretation. Why do we need an interpretation of the verses as contained in *The Geeta*? The verses are meant to be read, absorbed, felt, and followed, and one would need an enlightened Master or *Guru* to guide followers. Even the Masters differ while explaining the teachings of the scripture, and who am I to utter the final words? I have no intention to start an exclusive lineage of devotees, come on!

Scripture does not allow one to be judgmental. Scriptural verses deserve contemplation, and *Reflections on Salvation* is a work of literature, spread across eighteen short chapters, which hopefully stir the age-old notion about sacrifice, renunciation and salvation.

Kiriti Sengupta
June, 2016
Calcutta

[The introductory chapter first appeared at *The Huffington Post.*]

Publisher's Note

Reflections on Salvation is a collection of anecdotal wisdom that serves to both illuminate and discuss the paradox of faith. Sengupta boldly proclaims at the beginning that he has no intention of towing the standard line and he is perfectly at ease with loose interpretation. He denies rebirth and considers the senses the source of salvation. Here, we see a mind grappling with eccentric paradoxes presented in India's most elusive Scriptural text, and coming to the conclusion that rebirth comes from awareness within. Jesus Christ is recorded as saying, "The Kingdom of Heaven is within you." All things of reflection must be turned on their heads at some point, and Sengupta valiantly uses Scriptural texts to turn the afterlife upside down. This collection of reflections modernizes religious devotion.

Everyday reality is saturated with demands to be silent, to succumb to the public face. There is a need to maintain a relationship of honesty with oneself and cultivate self-love. Our world swamps us with hedonism, lies, self-deceit, vacant gestures...we aren't left with moments to be self-honest or relaxed. *Reflections on Salvation* reminds us of the humor in life and the opportunities such humor provides. While we are told life isn't all frivolity and games, we are freed to be modest and powerfully honest with ourselves without demeaning others or degrading our perceptions.

Tradition allows us to be flexible and gives us a ground to stand on. Without this ground, we are merely jumping off a precipice with no aim in mind. To move forward, one must have come from the past. This small collection of doubts, questions, and reflections is aimed at those who feel our traditions are too narrow and not contemporary enough to speak to the modern mind.

Dustin Pickering
July 20, 2016
Founder, Transcendent Zero Press
Houston, Texas

Acknowledgements

I'm thankful to Mary Torregrossa, who spent much time on the manuscript and suggested corrections, changes, and offered her valuable insights.

Eternally grateful to my Guru, Yogacharya Ashoke Kumar Chatterjee, who has enabled me to understand *The Geeta* in the light of Kriyayoga.

Many thanks to Dr. Casey Dorman who appreciated my effort and gladly wrote the foreword.

Hearty thanks to my wife, Bhaswati, and Aishikk, my son. They have always been extremely supportive and allowed me enough time to spend on writing.

My friends are the pillars of my life. Love to Prabir Roy, Shouvanik Dey Banerjee, Kaushik Acharya, Tanmoy Bhattacharjee and Pranab Ghosh.

I'm thankful to Transcendent Zero Press, especially Dustin Pickering, who considered the manuscript and agreed to publish my book.

Contents

Saffron

Why do we commission a priest to worship the household gods? I wonder if we are not capable enough to perform the action on our own. We are perhaps glued to the sacred thread, the holy *shaligram*, and we nurture the very thought of listening to the loud chants of the religious verses. Aren't we cursed badly by ourselves?

Saffron adds color and flavor to certain delicacies, but when it shows up on your attire, I find you saintly pious. It is all in my mind that has been grossly tuned to accept and refuse the effects of the colors they carry within.

I'm telling you, with saffron comes *sannyas* or renunciation, and with renunciation arrives attachment. Attachment with the world, attachment with domesticity, or may be the gods.

How does one become a monk? Is it by renouncing the fruits of actions one undertakes? Even the gods invite dependence, and remember, they are considered superior to the saints!

Mango

In India the mango is king of all fruits. Mangoes ripen to a ruby red with a hint of yellow and green peel. Inside the luscious pulp is sweet and glows the color of saffron. Ramakrishna says, "Your business is to eat mangoes ... go and eat them."*

Is it humanly possible to achieve renunciation? Why won't I dream of eating mangoes if I plant or even intend to plant a mango tree? Forget the tree, and think of fertilizers. They will only benefit as we sow a layer of seeds in the earth.

I expect patients in my clinic, and I expect them to listen to my advice. This is a fair deal, even *The Bible* wants its readers to become followers of Jesus!

[The Gospel of Sri Ramakrishna Vol 2: http://www.ramakrishnavivekananda.info/gospel/volume_2/34_b ankim_chandra.htm]

Payment

Necessity is the mother of invention, they say! You are one of the requisites the gods look out for; they need you to prosper further, and look, you plan to invent them through renunciation? Ask them instead to leave your earthly existence, and then, let them realize the value of attachment.

You seem to be hell-bent on relinquishing the cause-and-effect relationship. You work to get paid. Your family awaits funds on your payday. Does wisdom urge to neglect your loved ones? Did it not ask you to love your neighbors?

Conduct

Schools have their distinctive dress codes, and so do the religious sects. White, red, or saffron clad people fetch attention. With attention comes attachment; here renunciation is a far cry from living a life of an ascetic!

You never know, your next-door-neighbor, who works fulltime to earn a living and provides for his ailing mother, can well be a wise man, a true renunciate. And the man in question bothers the least to wear a robe that might loudly announce his achievement of renunciation.

Adhering to a particular code is probably a manifestation of failure; failure to secure non-attachment. Divinity might be found in conduct, but not in the codes. Understanding the objective of life, or the purpose of your worldly existence is your first step to reach the gods.

Stagecraft

Lights, camera, action! The spot boy uses a clapstick while the director utters these words. The actors deliver what they were asked to do. They follow their director, and at times improvise their actions.

You perform and we call it a performance. Shakespeare said, "All the world's a stage." What if you have no audience?

What if you are not applauded? You might blame your luck, but did you deliver your best? Salvation is but enlightenment, achievable only by actions, and through your sensory gateways.

Pleasure of exploring and realizing the unknown arrives only through the eyes, ears, nose, tongue, or skin.

Third Molar

A woman came to my clinic with a carious wisdom tooth. She had severe pain and wanted immediate relief. I made the tooth numb by lignocaine. Once relieved the woman became insistent and said that she wanted to save the affected tooth. I had to decline and prescribed a few medicines that would eliminate inflammation in the first place. I advised her to return after five days and get her tooth removed. She didn't agree and named a few modern procedures that might help her. She even questioned my skill, "Aren't you aware of atraumatic restorative treatment?"

I could not help it; I smiled and said, "Trauma necessarily precedes wisdom!"

Attachment

Smoking causes cancer. Smoking kills. Smoking will cost you.

You are a heavy smoker, but I told you these lines. I will make sure you have a few packs of cigarettes handy. I know, you have promised your wife that you won't smoke anymore. You are faithful to her, who is a little less appealing than your addiction to tobacco.

"Let me enjoy a last puff," you gushed!

Cow

An astrologer advised me to donate a few lactating cows to our family priest. He thinks by donating cows I will be able to get rid of my acquired sins and eventually I will please the gods, securing prosperity, wealth and peace.

I bought two cows and gave them to the priest. He appeared very happy and blessed me, "I'm delighted and so are the gods."

Although I followed the astrologer, my luck has not changed yet; our priest seems disappointed as those cows have stopped giving milk.

If scriptures are made for the humans, what about humanity?

Fire

You think of *yajña*, you consider liberation; but, I think of the amount of *ghee* it consumes, I think of the number of trees it kills. *The Vedas* did not count on malnutrition; they did not even consider environment, let alone poverty.

I wonder, Vedic scriptures have been written by a group of wise men who never lived on this earth! How would two give birth to one when they are poles apart?

Meditation

Take a chill pill! You glance through various self-help books as you mug up the steps of meditation. You have become aware of its benefits lately and you want to do it to still your mind.

Inside a darkened room you, step one, sit on a mat. Close your eyes, and think of doing *dhyana*.

Your legs ache, your neck stiffens, your body shivers, and you face a hell of a lot of troubles. You may wish to switch on the television and watch your favorite soap. What is the deadline of your thesis-submission? The cellular service provider sends you a reminder to pay up your outstanding bill to ensure uninterrupted service. But, if you stop meditating, you are only giving up your zeal to carry it on. *The Geeta* warns, "Benefits would be nullified!"

Who has been advocating detachment down the ages, by the way?

Paradise

No matter if you sacrifice your sweat and blood, or feel exhausted, you are to consider yourself duty-bound. You have to perform *yajña,* you have to donate and meditate. Bhabapagla, the great philosopher, might have connected beauty to duty, but did he count on our appearance?*

Roma spent her life on us — her children, husband, and her teaching career. Family has always been her first priority. She neglected her health, ignored her minimal desires and dreams, and served her family at all events. Ma is suffering from psoriasis for more than a decade now and she hates to step out under the sun. She does not look pretty anymore; her skin is patchy, it itches, oozes blood, and aches. My mother continues to serve her family even now. I therefore ask of Bhabapagla, is Roma headed for heaven because of duty or because of beauty?

[Doctrines of Bhabapagla: http://bhabapagla.com/doctrins.htm]

Return

Enough you said about getting rid of expectations, didn't you? A renunciate visits my neighborhood every Sunday and he knocks on every possible door for alms. He routinely says, "We have a small house for the *sadhus*, and we need generous donations for our living." I'm aware of a few families who give away funds to the monks and carefully preserve the receipts of their donation.

Donors are proud owners of such receipts as those are useful to claim income-tax-exemption. A formally printed donation-receipt in India is but a memoir of section 80G!

Another thought: A renunciate abandons the family — the root and the society, but comes back to them to secure living. Is the monk honest enough to be named a *sadhu*?

Krishna

We won't be bound by our actions; good or bad — we aren't the doers. So, when I'm worshipping the gods, they are, in fact, worshipping themselves. Why would I let that happen? I would rather worship myself and be happy. My physical frame, words I utter, and my mind — they have one thing in common: "I."

No matter if someone indulges in an unfair deed, the gods would suffer through us, and thus, we would remain unaffected. Did you hear me? You might call me ignorant, but I'm neither Krishna nor your beloved political servant.

Detachment

Marriages are made in heaven. But then, they too are expectant! Why won't a couple dream of being parents to their child if they are capable of giving birth to a new life?

On a serious note, I'm planning to donate a few copies of *The Geeta* to infertility clinics. I would love to hear them advising: "Act, but forget!" *The Geeta* says, "*karmaṇy-evādhikāras te mā phaleṣhu kadāchana/ mā karma-phala-hetur bhūr mā te saṅgo 'stvakarmaṇi* [You have a right to perform your duties, but you are not entitled to the fruits of your actions. Never consider yourself to be the cause of the results of your activities, nor be attached to inaction.*]."

But, did I consider how would a childless couple react to it? Situations change, but scriptures remain the same. Mundane!

[*The Geeta* Chapter 2, Verse 47]

14

Bondage

Even an ovum awaits communion to become a zygote. The organ gives birth and sacrifices one after another, and if not fertilized, they flow away from the tract. You call it monthly departure, but I would rather name it "link failure."

Release

We never spoke face-to-face, but thoughts surfaced on the line of our virtual friendship. Jayati, my friend, who has witnessed many worldly exits in her family life, thinks salvation is but releasing someone from a bondage and being happy! Jayati says, "*Moksha* is to let go!" Insightful indeed!

If salvation is the goal, spontaneity is the key!

[Jayati Mukherjee lives in Mumbai, India and she is working for human resources in a multinational company.]

Instinct

Maledictions help in achieving salvation. I'm not making fun, but you must keep it on your mind that Jara killed Krishna in a forest; a lethal arrow pierced into Krishna's foot that gave Jara an impression of a deer. I have no idea whether Jara considered himself the doer, or if it had been the gods who killed Krishna, the one who gathered many curses in his lifetime. Verse 17 of the concluding chapter of *The Geeta* says: "One who is not motivated by false ego, whose intelligence is not entangled, though he kills men in this world, is not the slayer. Nor is he bound by his actions."

Salman* is yet to get relieved from a lawsuit for having allegedly shot blackbucks in 1998. Killers deserve leniency — I wonder if the court is against the Lord.

[*Salman Khan is a renowned Indian actor.]

Salvation

Does one receive the gods? Even if they exist on the planet, I'll preferably inquire: "Get me the total headcount!" I can hear as someone murmurs, "God is one and amorphous." See, it is the God who claims: "*sarva-dharmān parityajya/ mām ekaṁ śaraṇaṁ vraja... [Abandon all religions and take refuge in me...*]*."

We live as long as we breathe; and it is but the breathing which occurs on its own will. No gods, but the breath that builds a home for our life and death.

They say, God dwells within; it is then the mortal exploration of the resort where salvation is largely seen!

[*The Geeta chapter 18, verse 66]

18

Epilogue

Postscript

I tend to believe that everyone at some point in their lives questions the beliefs and dogmas of the religion they have been brought up with. What Kiriti Sengupta does here with his work *Reflections on Salvation* is to reflect upon the teachings of The Geeta, the Hindu text in the Vedic tradition. He seems most concerned with the concept of renunciation or *sanyas*, which in Hinduism is the hallmark of spiritual life, but involves withdrawing into oneself, and removal of all attachments to the outside world.

The concepts of asceticism and monasticism themselves may seem a bit foreign, especially to Western readers, as there is little that is comparable in the Christian-Judeo traditions largely found here, at least not in the secular sense. Kiriti does however take a thought provoking approach to his analysis, which may inspire the reader to do the same, and not just in areas related to religion and spirituality. His assessments often explore the relationship between renunciation, and the resulting detachment from the things people most enjoy in the real world, when it's those very attachments that may in fact bring the most joy and salvation for many. He acknowledges his thoughts and words are often in conflict with his peers and religious scholars, but he argues *"Salvation is but enlightenment, achievable only by actions, and through your sensory gateways. Pleasure of exploring and realizing the unknown arrives only*

I

through the eyes, ears, nose, tongue, or skin."

Another concept that Kiriti touches on, and may be more familiar to Western readers, is the idea that religious texts are even relevant in the modern world. Most were written hundreds, if not thousands of years ago, and their authors could not have begun to predict the many changes over the years, and the complex society we live in today. Certainly most of us, if not all, have had similar thoughts, and Kiriti is quick to acknowledge his interpretations of things are no more valid than anyone else's. In the end though, this short work by Kiriti Sengupta provides a reflective contemplation on the role of religion, and its relationship to its followers in today's society.

Alan W. Jankowski
July 19, 2016
Parlin, New Jersey

Dustin Pickering interviews Kiriti Sengupta

The interview first appeared in *The Statesman* under the title "No alien in America" on March 6, 2016.

[http://www.thestatesman.com/news/8th-day/no-alien-in-america/128046.html]

Kiriti Sengupta is the author of *A Freshman's Welcome*; the bestselling trilogy: *My Glass of Wine*, *The Reverse Tree*, and *Healing Waters Floating Lamps*; and recently, *The Earthen Flute*. *The Earthen Flute* is a bestselling collection in America in Indian literature. Sengupta works in Calcutta in dentistry and likes to nurture friendships with younger writers. Dustin Pickering, editor-in-chief of *Harbinger Asylum*, caught him in a moment of contemplation after his newest book hit the shelves.

What inspires you the most to continue writing?

My studies, observations and living! If you want me to elaborate on them, it will take pages, but I would like to state that I study to observe, and I observe to reflect on my studies. I am no way close to what you say as "ideal living," and I truly look out for holistic living measures. You know, we often talk about "evidence-based-dentistry," and my life essentially complies with living evidences. Honestly, it is the deviation from the set-rules that keeps me going.

Do you set aside a time for writing? Is there a moment in your daily activities when you feel most inspired?

Nothing like that. My friends consider me happy-go-lucky kind of a guy! People often say, "You don't look like a writer, let alone a poet." I appreciate their views, and unless I feel like pouring out my words I don't write even an update on Facebook. I don't enjoy a set time that I can devote to my writing. I am a practicing dental surgeon, I manage a small press as well. I meet authors and poets on and off. And yes, I don't socialize as it is expected from a family person. I don't write on a daily basis, but my mind quickly registers the observations, which let me thrive on them.

What is your daily life like? Does it get entwined with your poetry?

I have a day job, Dustin. As I said before I practice as a dental surgeon, and there are but a few occasions when poetry occurs. Do you remember the poem "Envy" in my latest collection, *The Earthen Flute*? It got humor, it also bore sarcasm. Above all, "Envy" could be treated as psychosomatic poetry, but readers might consider it weird. Listen to these lines, and I hope you won't mind:

> *Jealous—*
> *A Dentist can say if you are one*
>
> *Your teeth deviate from*
> *The occlusal table*
> *And thus, lips suffer from bites*

Is there a place for poetry and literature in India's

popular imagination? It seems Americans find it dull and tedious.

Poetry is popular only among poets, worldwide! One who appreciates poetry writes poetry. He/she may not be a published poet, but then you need not to write a poem on a paper, or on your cellphone to establish your claim of being a poet. What name would you like to offer to someone who continues to write poetry in his/her mind? There are numerous such people, and they hardly wish to be marked as poet. I'll love to call them "non-practicing poets." And poetry essentially thrives on both the practicing and non-practicing group of poets.

India is considered the spiritual capital of the world. We got innumerable sages and monks who had made verses popular in our land. And then, we had Tagore, who made global readers serious about Bengali poetry. Poetry is an extremely important ingredient of Indian culture and philosophy. The corporate India may not be interested in literature or poetry, but they don't govern our heritage in any capacity.

In America, we host "slams": poetry competitions based on performance. This seems to be the most popular outlet for poetry's expression. Does India have a specific outlet poetry finds itself in?

Honestly, I am not aware of poetry competitions in India. We have a few important literary festivals that happen annually, but I don't think they dedicate even half of their tenure to poetry. Probably in all major cities we have groups of poets, but then I wonder, if they are, in any way, instrumental in bringing out quality poetry.

Tell me about your upcoming collection. Is there a message you wish to convey? Who are you addressing your words to?

My newest book of poems is titled *The Earthen Flute*. Kolkata based Hawakal Publisher has published and launched it formally on Feb 21 (2016) in Calcutta. My poetry essentially bears messages that I wish to convey to my readers. But I am not the right person to state those messages, for poetry is reader-specific. There are twenty-one poems in this book; short, long and prose-poems. A few of them have appeared in literary journals and blogs. I have added fresh poems as well. There are illustrations that add to the appeal. All in all, *The Earthen Flute*, I'm pretty sure, is going to be a collector's edition. Truth-seekers and poetry lovers around the world may find my work worthy! You will be glad to know that my book has been reviewed on *The Lake* magazine (United Kingdom) even before its release. You may read the complete preview on this link:

http://www.thelakepoetry.co.uk/reviews/february16/

The *Millennium Post* (English daily published both in Calcutta and New Delhi) said:

> In this collection of 21 poems, Sengupta talks about how the modern youth is obsessed by what is trendy but ignorant about the wisdom that ancient mythology is laden with. "For example, in a poem titled "Cryptic Idioms," I talk about how we follow certain yogic postures without even realizing that these were actually part of Sanatan Dharma or Hindu mythology," Sengupta told *Millennium Post*.

Do you feel your poetry is more personal or transcendent? If personal, how does the average reader relate? If transcendent, how do you reach that state?

If my poetry is personal or transcendent, critics can answer this best. I don't write poetry to make it personal or the other way round. I try to convey messages. Some call them "wisdom messages," others may term my poetry surrealistic! I'm not bothered, you see. I remain conscious when I compose a poem, but poetry essentially arrives without a notice. Let me quote a few lines from a critique:

> If Sengupta were to follow T.S. Eliot's dictum that true art should be impersonal, what would that lead to? The clash of opinions still persists — that between the romantic school and the modernist school — Sengupta adheres to the romantic school of thought. It's the creator's choice and I guess it's right for him because if he were to turn impersonal, that would take away the essence of his signature poems, the unique subjective and personal elements. (Page 33, Ketaki Datta and Tania Chakravertty/*Rhapsodies and Musings*/ Hawakal Publishers/ July 2015)

I can remember a commentary on my trilogy:

> Worldly observations become the occasion for explorations of meanings: of the self and its status within the world and within consciousness, and of life's journey from birth to death ... While Sengupta's poems touch the spirit, and often deal with spiritual matters, they are uniformly grounded in the world

around us. (Casey Dorman/ *The Statesman*/ Jan 31, 2016)

What characterizes a good poet from a bad one? Are there objective criteria? Can habit make a person a poet? What distinguishes a poet from one who writes poetry?

These are difficult to answer, Dustin! You have added so many brief questions together. Who is a poet, if I may ask? One may be a famous poet, a popular poet, an esteemed poet, an unknown poet, a non-practicing poet, but they all are poets in the first place. They are neither good, nor are they bad. You love a poet, but then do you love all his/her poems? I mean, all poems that he/she writes? You read a not-so-good poem, written by your beloved poet; how would you rate/grade the poet now? When can a writer claim him/her-self as a poet? I never claim myself as a poet. I write poetry, and if I can be named "poet" is to be ascertained by my readers and reviewers. Don't go by the dictionary and name a writer "poet" if he/she writes poetry.

How do you find the time to write?

How do you manage time to eat, Dustin? Aren't you too occupied to manage even a nap? You are to eat and sleep and write. And I am no exception. Hey, did I answer your question?

Do you think the "Muse" is a real being? What purpose does she serve? Who is she? Why does she latch onto certain people?

Do you think the "Muse" is a female being? Why do you think so? The "Muse" is only you, if you understand my point. Let me quote a few lines from *The Earthen Flute*.

VIII

I'm not a pervert, take a note!
I'm a woman as long as I'm dynamic
I'm a woman unless I'm stilled
Do you think of a woman's voyage to the heaven?
("Seventh Heaven")

The "Muse" is only your kinetic mind. Your soul keeps wandering to understand the reason(s) of being restless over the years. And it is the "Muse" that allows one to pen down the thoughts of restlessness. You cannot appreciate quietude by keeping mum. You would not be able to celebrate silence if you remain soundless. You have to cultivate the skill of becoming still. Tranquility has its charm when enjoyed in noise. A poet is the blessed soul who struggles for silence and peace, and thus guiding the society in a subtle way towards a harmonious cohabitation with the "Muse."

Do you read a lot? Does reading factor into your writing? What role does reading play for a writer? How much do you read on average?

I'm an average reader. Thanks to my lazy eyes that have made me one such. Long poems tire me, extremely long essays exhaust my brain to no end, and fat novels are too repulsive to sit on my desk. Reading influences the psyche, and thus your writing shows the signs of your reading habit. They say it is important to learn, and even more important to unlearn things.

Do you ever face adversity for being a writer? Are you humiliated or have you been unfairly criticized?

I have my share of negative reviews of my work, but then who I am to justify! I have never paid my reviewers, neither did I influence them in any way. Dustin, why don't you tell the world about how I managed the notes of appreciation (blurbs) from a few American poets in relation with *The Earthen Flute*? I was fairly surprised when both Jonathan Moody and Lorna Dee Cervantes wrote on my work, entirely based on the merit or quality of the manuscript.

I was bullied in school at times for being bookish and was considered a teacher's pet, and sometimes teachers themselves thought I was weird. I never fit in to the in-crowd. Years ago, I had a neighbor who believed people who read were ugly and stupid. He insisted that on his trips to the library, he saw only old people or ugly women. It was extremely insulting, but I practiced my usual "Christian forbearance" and was kind until he was evicted from the apartment complex for assaulting me (after a long series of mishaps, the manager was tired of him as well). I think with a head of tough wisdom (not the earthly kind, but philosophical like Ecclesiastes) you are bound to writhe some days. I haven't had harsh critiques from publishers or reviewers, and most other poets have a favorable attitude toward my writing. This has been a life-long pursuit for me, beginning when I wrote a short story called *The Little Red Wagon*, written from a child's imagination. The story was about a young man who loses a wheel off his wagon, and searches for it all day only to find it at the day's end where he least expects it. I developed a strong sense of the calling at a young age, taking advice from my grandmother on both reading habits and approaches to writing. In your opinion, what is the greatest thing to be proud of as a poet?

Honestly, I have no idea. You know, I once asked Bibhas Roy Chowdhury about why a poet feels insulted when he/she is referred to as writer. He told me, "Poet is the highest adjective available to a writer."

What other writers you admire? Who is currently on you "to read" list?

I have a long list that starts with Tagore and ends with you, Dustin. I would prefer not to take their names, for they are admired on the basis of their poetry. I'm now reading two books: *When God Is A Traveller* by Arundhathi Subramaniam, and *The Daunting Ephemeral*.

Does writing serve a purpose for non-writers? Comedian Jerry Seinfeld once said the secret to his success was writing every day. How do you think writing can help those who aren't writers?

Ask a psychotherapist and you will understand how writing helps an individual in his/her day-to-day life. Writing helps in more than one way to combat stress, depression and mental blockage. I must tell you, Dustin, I used to write uncountable love-letters to my girl-friend who is now my wife.

What is literacy like in India? What type of literature does the average Indian read?

India is no exception, we love to value fiction stories more than any other genre of literature.

Finally, is there still a sense of the sacred in India where much of the sacred was born?

India is a holy land; the land of spirituality. Even now we have a handful of realized souls, and I am proud to have been associated with a few of those Masters.

www.ingramcontent.com/pod-product-compliance
Lightning Source LLC
Chambersburg PA
CBHW030526130626
46549CB00007B/3121